THE **TRANSFORMERS**

DRIFT

THE TRANSFORMERS DRIFT

WRITTEN BY
SHANE MCCARTHY

ART BY
ALEX MILNE

COLORS BY
JOSH PEREZ

LETTERS BY
CHRIS MOWRY & SHAWN LEE

SERIES EDITOR:
DENTON J. TIPTON

CONSULTING EDITOR:
ANDY SCHMIDT

COLLECTION DESIGN:
CHRIS MOWRY

COLLECTION EDITS:
JUSTIN EISINGER

COVER ARTWORK BY ALEX MILNE
COVER COLORS BY JOSH PEREZ

Licensed By:

Special thanks to Hasbro's Aaron Archer, Michael Kelly, Amie Lozanski, Ed Lane, Michael Provost, Val Roca, Erin Hillman, Jos Huxley, Samantha Lomow, and Michael Verrecchia for their invaluable assistance.

www.IDWPUBLISHING.com   ISBN: 978-1-60010-855-6   14 13 12 11   1 2 3 4

IDW Publishing is: Operations: Ted Adams, CEO & Publisher • Greg Goldstein, Chief Operating Officer • Matthew Ruzicka, CPA, Chief Financial Officer • Alan Payne, VP of Sales • Lorelei Bunjes, Director of Digital Services • Jeff Webber, Director of ePublishing • AnnaMaria White, Dir., Marketing and Public Relations • Dirk Wood, Dir., Retail Marketing • Marci Hubbard, Executive Assistant • Alonzo Simon, Shipping Manager • Angela Loggins, Staff Accountant • Cherrie Go, Assistant Web Designer • Editorial: Chris Ryall, Chief Creative Officer, Editor-In-Chief • Scott Dunbier, Senior Editor, Special Projects • Andy Schmidt, Senior Editor • Justin Eisinger, Senior Editor, Books • Kris Oprisko, Editor/Foreign Lic. • Denton J. Tipton, Editor • Tom Waltz, Editor • Mariah Huehner, Editor • Carlos Guzman, Assistant Editor • Bobby Curnow, Assistant Editor • Design: Robbie Robbins, EVP/Sr. Graphic Artist • Neil Uyetake, Senior Art Director • Chris Mowry, Senior Graphic Artist • Amauri Osorio, Graphic Artist • Gilberto Lazcano, Production Assistant • Shawn Lee, Graphic Artist